KEEP CALM AND PRAY

✝

KEEP
CALM
AND
PRAY

Andrews McMeel Publishing, LLC
an Andrews McMeel Universal company
1130 Walnut Street, Kansas City, Missouri 64106

www.andrewsmcmeel.com

15 16 17 18 19 TEN 10 9 8 7 6 5 4 3 2 1

ISBN: 978-1-4494-7202-3

Published by arrangement with Summersdale Publishers Ltd.
With research by Caroline Hodgson

ATTENTION: SCHOOLS AND BUSINESSES
Andrews McMeel books are available at quantity discounts
with bulk purchase for educational, business, or sales promotional use.
For information, please e-mail the Andrews McMeel Publishing
Special Sales Department: specialsales@amuniversal.com.

✝

KEEP
CALM
AND
PRAY

Andrews McMeel
Publishing®

Kansas City • Sydney • London

Disturb us, Lord,
to dare more boldly,
To venture on wider seas
Where storms will show
your mastery;
Where losing sight of land,
We shall find stars.

Francis Drake

*Prepare the way of the Lord,
make his paths straight.*

Matthew 3:3

Truth and Love are wings that cannot be separated, for Truth cannot fly without Love, nor can Love soar aloft without Truth; their yoke is one of amity.

Ephrem the Syrian

So if anyone is in Christ, there is a new creation: everything old has passed away; see, everything has become new!

2 Corinthians 5:17

We are not human beings having a spiritual experience; we are spiritual beings having a human experience.

Pierre Teilhard de Chardin

*For it was you who
formed my inward parts;
you knit me together in
my mother's womb.
I praise you, for I am fearfully
and wonderfully made.*

Psalm 139:13–14

Your hand
upholds the universe,
Your love gives rest
to the world.

Cyrillona

See, I am sending you
out like sheep into the
midst of wolves; so be wise
as serpents and innocent
as doves.

Matthew 10:16

Thank God every morning when you get up that you have something to do that day which must be done, whether you like it or not.

Charles Kingsley

Our salvation is in loving
and cherishing his creation,
in so living that others
may have life.

Gerard W. Hughes

Most merciful Redeemer,
Friend, and Brother,
may we know you
more clearly,
love you more dearly,
and follow you more nearly,
day by day.

Richard of Chichester

Endeavor seven times
a day to withdraw from
business and company
and lift up thy soul to God
in private retirement.

Adoniram Judson

The lark's on the wing;
The snail's on the thorn;
God's in his heaven—
All's right with the world!

Robert Browning

. . . and what does the Lord require of you but to do justice, and to love kindness, and to walk humbly with your God?

Micah 6:8

O God, to those who have hunger, give bread, and to us who have bread, give the hunger for justice.

Latin American prayer

I worry until midnight and from then on I let God worry.

Luigi Guanella

God is our refuge and strength,
a very present help in trouble.

Psalm 46:1

The glory of Christianity is to conquer by forgiveness.

William Blake

Forgiving is not forgetting;
it's actually remembering—
remembering and not using your
right to hit back.

Desmond Tutu

*Teach us, good Lord,
to serve you as you deserve,
to give and not to count the cost…
save that of knowing
that we do your will.*

Ignatius of Loyola

When He tells us
to love our enemies,
He gives, along with the
command, the love itself.

Corrie ten Boom

Blessed are the merciful,
for they will receive mercy.
Blessed are the pure in heart,
for they will see God.

Matthew 5:7–8

No pain, no palm; no thorns, no throne . . .

William Penn

Breathe on me,
Breath of God,
Fill me with life anew,
That I may love what
thou dost love,
And do what thou
wouldst do.

Edwin Hatch

The darker the night—
the brighter the stars,
The deeper the grief—
the closer is God!

Fyodor Dostoyevsky

When we are nothing,
we are in a fine position
to receive everything
from God.

Richard Rohr

*. . . give us the true
courage which shows
itself by gentleness; the true
wisdom which shows itself by
simplicity; and the true power
which shows itself
by modesty.*

Charles Kingsley

We are closest to God
in the darkness,
stumbling along blindly.

Madeleine L'Engle

For most of us the prayer in Gethsemane is the only model. Removing mountains can wait.

C. S. Lewis

The function of prayer is
not to influence God,
but rather to change the nature
of the one who prays.

Søren Kierkegaard

As he went ashore,
he saw a great crowd;
and he had compassion for them,
because they were like sheep
without a shepherd; and he began
to teach them . . .

Mark 6:34

*God be in my heart,
and in my thinking;
God be at my end,
and at my departing.*

The Sarum Primer

If I speak in the tongues
of mortals and of angels,
but do not have love,
I am a noisy gong or
a clanging cymbal.

1 Corinthians 13:1

God is silent,
now if we can only
get man to shut up.

Woody Allen

Little children, keep yourselves from idols.

1 John 5:21

Keep awake and pray
that you may not come into
the time of trial; the spirit indeed
is willing, but the flesh is weak.

Mark 14:38

No point in becoming a saint
by halves. I'm not afraid of
suffering for your sake;
the only thing I'm afraid of is
clinging to my own will.

Thérèse of Lisieux

Be a sinner and sin boldly, but believe and rejoice in Christ even more boldly.

Martin Luther

Whoever does the will of God is my brother and sister and mother.

Mark 3:35

Where you go, I will go:
where you lodge,
I will lodge;
your people shall
be my people,
and your God my God.

Ruth 1:16

If you want to make
God laugh, tell him
about your plans.

Woody Allen

Your hand has been over me and has guarded and preserved me.

Dietrich Bonhoeffer

God will not look you over
for medals, degrees, or
diplomas, but for scars.

Elbert Hubbard

So we can say with confidence,
"The Lord is my helper;
I will not be afraid. What can
anyone do to me?"

Hebrews 13:6

I sought to hear the
voice of God and climbed
the topmost steeple,
but God declared:
"Go down again—I dwell
among the people."

John Henry Newman

*Let the night be too
dark for me to see
Into the future.
Let what will be, be.*

Robert Frost

Have you believed
because you have seen me?
Blessed are those who
have not seen and yet
have come to believe.

John 20:29

We may be surprised
at the people we find
in heaven. God has a
soft spot for sinners.

Desmond Tutu

*O Lord, help me
not to despise or oppose
what I do not understand.*

William Penn

God whispers to us in our pleasures, speaks in our consciences, but shouts in our pains.

C. S. Lewis

One shall not kill
"the evil impulse," the
passion, in oneself, but one
shall serve God *with it . . .*

Martin Buber

*Open wide the door of our hearts,
that we may receive and entertain
Thee with all our powers of
adoration and love. Amen.*

Christina Rossetti

. . . my flesh is frail and weak. If I therefore at any time forget thee, touch my heart, O Lord, that I may again remember thee.

Queen Elizabeth I

Blessed are those who hunger
and thirst for righteousness,
for they will be filled.

Matthew 5:6

Even though I walk through the darkest valley, I fear no evil, for you are with me; your rod and your staff—they comfort me.

Psalm 23:4

Had Mary been filled
with reason
There'd have been no
room for the child.

Madeleine L'Engle

He became what we are
that he might make us
what he is.

Athanasius of Alexandria

My soul magnifies the Lord,
and my spirit rejoices
in God my Savior,
for he has looked with
favor on the lowliness
of his servant.

Luke 1:46–48

The Bible without the
Holy Spirit is a sundial
by moonlight.

Dwight L. Moody

Arise, shine; for your light has come, and the glory of the Lord has risen upon you.

Isaiah 60:1

Dear Lord, be good to me. The sea is so wide, and my boat is so small.

Prayer of an Irish fisherman

God is the only one who
can make the valley of trouble
a door of hope.

Catherine Marshall

Behold, miracle of miracles,
out of the cracks a
light shines.

Choan-Seng Song

You will pray to him,
and he will hear you . . .

Job 22:27

The most difficult and decisive part of prayer is acquiring this ability to listen. Listening is no passive affair.

Mother Mary Clare SLG

Thou, O Lord, that stillest the raging of the sea, hear, hear us, and save us . . .

The Book of Common Prayer

So begin: and continually repeat and repeat, but all the time keep before you the thought of our Lord.

Theophan the Recluse, on prayer

Just as the eye perceives
light and the ear sound,
the heart is the organ
for meaning.

David Steindl-Rast

Ask, and it will be given you;
search and you will find;
knock, and the door will
be opened for you.

Matthew 7:7

Joy runs deeper
than despair.

Corrie ten Boom

*Oh, God of dust
and rainbows,
help us see
That without
dust the rainbow
would not be.*

Langston Hughes

And when it rains on your parade,
look up rather than down.
Without the rain, there would
be no rainbow.

G. K. Chesterton

Darkness cannot
drive out darkness:
only light can do that.
Hate cannot drive out hate:
only love can do that.

Martin Luther King, Jr.

If I love until it hurts,
then there is
no hurt, but only
more love.

Daphne Rae

*God, give me grace to accept
with serenity the things that
cannot be changed,
Courage to change the things
which should be changed,
and the Wisdom to distinguish
the one from the other.*

Reinhold Niebuhr

If you have never
had any distractions
you don't know
how to pray.

Thomas Merton

If you plan to build a high house of virtues, you must first lay deep foundations of humility.

Augustine of Hippo

Prayer is nothing else than being on terms of friendship with God.

Teresa of Avila

Pray as you can,
and don't try to pray
as you can't!

John Chapman

. . . let me see thee face to face . . . thou dearest Jesus, whom my soul longeth after.

William Romaine

God sends no one away empty except those who are full of themselves.

Dwight L. Moody

It is a splendid habit to laugh
inwardly at yourself.
It is the best way of regaining your
good humor and of finding God
without further anxiety.

Henri de Tourville

There is no limit that can be set to our growth in our Godward life, since the good has no limit . . .

Gregory of Nyssa

Whatever else I am dissatisfied with, there is One whom I can contemplate with utter satisfaction, and bathe my stained soul in that eternal fount of purity.

Charles Kingsley

They who have all that they want and desire, know joy. But no one has this except those whose will is one with God's will.

Meister Eckhart

I will thank him for the
pleasures given me through
my senses, for the glory of
the thunder, for the mystery
of music . . .

Edward King

*Grant me, O Lord,
a sunny mind . . .*

Emily Dickinson

For it is certain that whatever
seeming calamity happens to you,
if you thank and praise God for it,
you turn it into a blessing.

William Law

. . . the Lord gave, and
the Lord has taken away;
blessed be the name
of the Lord.

Job 1:21

The tears of our own grief
can soften our hardened hearts
and open us to the possibility
to say "thanks."

Henri Nouwen

*I shall revive at thy light;
my vital spirits will confess thy
presence. Grief and anxiety will
vanish before thee, and immortal
joys surround my soul.*

Elizabeth Rowe

You can do very little
with faith, but you can do
nothing without it.

Samuel Butler

Human beings must be known to be loved, but divine things must be loved to be known.

Blaise Pascal, paraphrased

Understanding is the reward of faith. Therefore, seek not to understand that thou mayest believe, but believe that thou mayest understand.

Augustine of Hippo

. . . in prosperity prayers seem
but a mere medley of words,
until misfortune comes and the
unhappy sufferer first understands
the meaning of the sublime
language . . .

Alexandre Dumas

I've read the last page
of the Bible. It's all going
to turn out all right.

Billy Graham

Be still, and know that I am God!

Psalm 46:10

The fear of the Lord is
the beginning of knowledge;
fools despise wisdom
and instruction.

Proverbs 1:7

It is perfectly evident to my mind that there exists a necessary, eternal, supreme, and intelligent being. This is no matter of faith, but of reason.

Voltaire

*My spirit longs
for Thee,
Within my
troubled breast,
Though I unworthy be
Of so divine a guest.*

John Byrom

God instructs the heart,
not by ideas but by pains
and contradictions.

Jean Pierre de Caussade

When He plans
to plant a garden,
He starts in the desert.

Patricia St. John

*Teach me, O God . . .
to breathe deeply
in faith.*

Søren Kierkegaard

Make sure you are
doing what God wants
you to do—then do it
with all your strength.

George Washington

No man can be called
friendless who has God
and the companionship
of good books.

Elizabeth Barrett Browning

*As the first Adam's
sweat surrounds my face,
May the last Adam's blood
my soul embrace.*

John Donne

*O Jesus, I have promised
To serve thee to the end;
Be thou for ever near me,
My Master and my Friend . . .*

John E. Bode

Let us take things
as we find them: let us not
attempt to distort them
into what they are not . . .
We cannot make facts . . .
We must use them.

John Henry Newman

. . . it is in the unclouded night-sky, where His worlds wheel their silent course, that we read clearest His infinitude, His omnipotence, His omnipresence.

Charlotte Brontë

If God were not willing to forgive sin, heaven would be empty.

German proverb

Lord Jesus Christ,
Son of God,
have mercy on me,
a sinner.

The Jesus Prayer

Eternity is not something that
begins after you are dead.
It is going on all the time.
We are in it now.

Charlotte Perkins Gilman

God loves each of us as if there were only one of us.

Augustine of Hippo

God is closer to us than
our own soul, for he is
the foundation on which
our soul stands . . .

Julian of Norwich

Earth's crammed with heaven,
And every common bush
afire with God;
And only he who sees
takes off his shoes—
The rest sit round it and
pluck blackberries . . .

Elizabeth Barrett Browning

*Alone with none
but thee, my God,
I journey on my way.
What need I fear when
thou art near,
O king of night
and day?*

Columba

Come down, O love divine,
Seek thou this soul of mine,
And visit it with thine own
ardor glowing . . .

Bianco da Siena

By perseverance the snail
reached the ark.

Charles Spurgeon

Stupidity is also a gift
of God, but one mustn't
misuse it.

Pope John Paul II

I would rather say five words
devoutly with my heart,
than five thousand which my
soul does not relish with affection
and understanding.

Edmund the Martyr

What I kept, I lost.
What I spent, I had.
What I gave, I have.

Persian proverb

But when we speak with God,
our power of addressing Him . . .
and listening to His still small
voice, depends on our will being
one and the same with His.

Florence Nightingale

One grain of love is better
than a hundredweight
of intellect.

Edward Bouverie Pusey

The capital of heaven is the heart in which Jesus is enthroned as King.

Sadhu Sundar Singh

Forth in thy Name,
O Lord, I go,
My daily labor to pursue;
Thee, only thee,
resolved to know,
In all I think or speak or do.

Charles Wesley

We can only know God well
by knowing our iniquities.
Therefore those who have
known God, without knowing
their wretchedness, have not
glorified Him, but have
glorified themselves.

Blaise Pascal

For everything
there is a season,
and a time for every matter
under heaven . . .

Ecclesiastes 3:1

*O Lord! thou knowest how busy
I must be this day;
if I forget thee, do not
thou forget me.*

**Jacob Astley, 1st Baron Astley of Reading
(before going into battle)**

Take heart, daughter;
your faith has
made you well.

Matthew 9:22

I have formerly lived
by hearsay and faith;
but now I go where I shall
live by sight, and shall be
with Him in whose company
I delight myself.

John Bunyan

*Lord, make me an instrument
of Your peace!
Where there is hatred,
let me sow love . . .
Where there
is darkness, light,
And where there
is sadness, joy.*

Francis of Assisi

Keep your lives free from the love of money, and be content with what you have; for he has said, "I will never leave you or forsake you."

Hebrews 13:5

Bestow upon me, O Lord my God, an understanding that knows thee, wisdom in finding thee . . . and confidence that I shall embrace thee at the last.

Thomas Aquinas

I will sing to my God
a new song: O Lord,
you are great and glorious,
wonderful in strength,
invincible.

Judith 16:13

For I am convinced that neither
death, nor life . . . nor things
present, nor things to come . . .
will be able to separate us from
the love of God . . .

Romans 8:38–39

Faith is the highest passion in a human being. Many in every generation may not come that far, but none comes further.

Søren Kierkegaard

In the midst of winter,
I found there was within me,
an invincible summer.

Albert Camus

When the solution is simple,
God is answering.

Albert Einstein

Grace is love that cares
and stoops and rescues.

John Stott

O thou lord of life,
send my roots rain.

Gerard Manley Hopkins

*Give me my
scallop-shell of quiet,
My staff of faith to
walk upon . . .
My gown of glory,
hope's true gage,
And thus I'll take my pilgrimage.*

Walter Raleigh

I fear God, yet I am not
afraid of Him.

Thomas Browne

In returning and rest you shall be saved; in quietness and in trust shall be your strength.

Isaiah 30:15

For now we see in a
mirror, dimly, but then we will
see face to face. Now
I know only in part; then
I will know fully . . .

1 Corinthians 13:12

*If I am in sickness, my sickness
may serve Him; in perplexity,
my perplexity may serve Him;
if I am in sorrow, my sorrow
may serve Him.*

John Henry Newman

Grace be with all
who have an undying love
for our Lord Jesus Christ.

Ephesians 6:24

Faith is awe in the presence of the divine incognito . . .

Karl Barth

All shall be well and all
shall be well and all manner
of thing shall be well.

Julian of Norwich

The world thirsts for grace.
When grace descends, the
world falls silent before it.

Philip Yancey

Tension, anxiety,
worry, frustration, all melt away
before him, as snow before
the sun.

Jim Borst

Always God is with us.
And, in the long run, that is
all we need to know.

David Watson

May He support us all the day long, till the shades lengthen, and the evening comes, and the busy world is hushed, and the fever of life is over, and our work is done!

John Henry Newman

And now faith, hope,
and love abide, these three;
and the greatest of these
is love.

1 Corinthians 13:13

I am the Alpha and the
Omega, the first and the
last, the beginning
and the end.

Revelation 22:13

KEEP KEEP KEEP KEEP
CALM CALM CALM CALM
AND AND AND AND
PRAY PRAY PRAY PRAY

KEEP KEEP KEEP KEEP
CALM CALM CALM CALM
AND AND AND AND AND
PRAY PRAY PRAY PRAY

KEEP KEEP KEEP KEEP
CALM CALM CALM CALM
AND AND AND AND
PRAY PRAY PRAY PRAY

KEEP KEEP KEEP KEEP
CALM CALM CALM CALM
AND AND AND AND
PRAY PRAY PRAY PRAY

KEEP KEEP KEEP KEEP
CALM CALM CALM CALM
AND AND AND AND AND
PRAY PRAY PRAY PRAY

KEEP KEEP KEEP KEEP
CALM CALM CALM CALM
AND AND AND AND